Look and Play
Giant Machines

by Jim Pipe

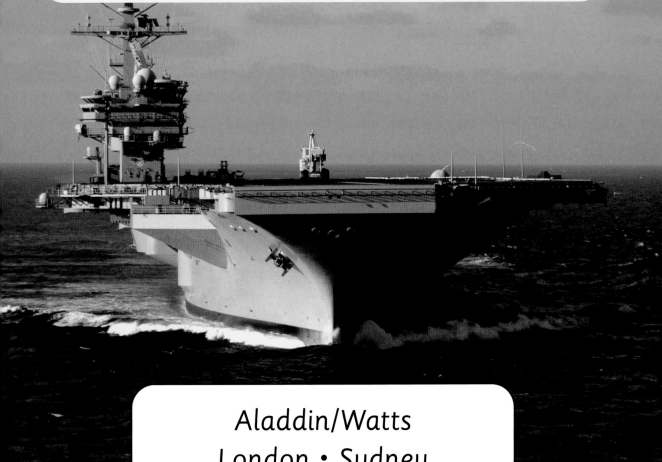

Aladdin/Watts
London • Sydney

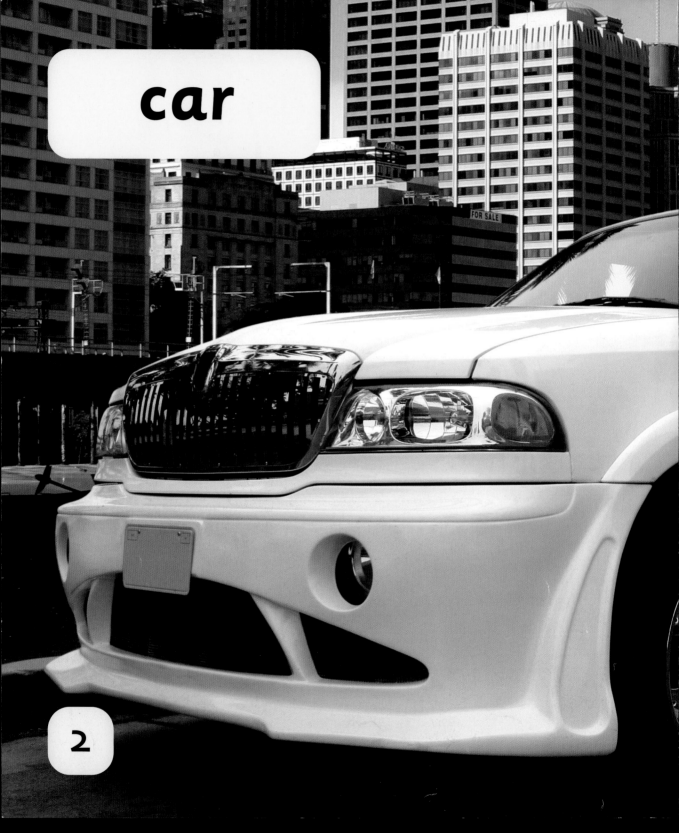

car

2

This giant **car** is very big!

truck

A giant **truck** is very heavy.

4

5

robot

6

This giant **robot** is scary!

helicopter

This **helicopter** is very strong.

8

9

submarine

This **submarine** is very long.

plane

This **plane** is very wide.

13

rocket

14

A **rocket** is very tall.

digger

This giant **digger** works fast.

16

17

ship

This giant **ship**
is long and wide.

19

What am I?

train

wheel

ship

tank

Match the words and pictures.

How many?

Can you count the big ships?

What noise?

Crunch!

Chucka!

Whoosh!

Roar!

Can you sound like these machines?

Index

For Parents and Teachers

Questions you could ask:

p. 2 How many people could fit in this car? This car, a Chrysler 300, is over 5 metres long and almost 2 metres wide. It can fit up to 16 passengers.

p. 4 Can you see the ladder? The truck is so big the driver needs a ladder to climb up into the cab. The truck works at a mine carrying heavy rocks.

p. 6 What does the giant robot look like? The 12-metre tall robot is built like a dragon (e.g. it breathes fire) and can crush a car in its claws.

p. 8 What is the helicopter doing? Point out the heavy load slung below the helicopter (a Chinook). It is carrying food and other supplies to people during a disaster.

p. 10 What can a submarine do? A submarine can travel underwater (for weeks at a time). Point out the crew on the deck to show the size of the vessel.

p. 12 Look at all the windows! This plane, an Airbus 380, can carry up to 555 passengers. It can fly almost 15,000 kilometres without stopping.

p. 14 What is carrying the rocket? A huge truck (the biggest in the world) carries the rocket to the launch pad. The man and van give a sense of scale.

p. 18 Can you see the swimming pool? This ship, the Seven Seas Voyager, is a floating hotel. Ships like this are the biggest machines in the world.

Activities you could do:

• Ask readers to describe or draw the biggest machine they have ever seen, e.g. comparing how large it is relative to other objects they know, how many people it carries, what it does etc.

• Go outside and ask readers to measure out how big the machines are, e.g. if one pace is 0.5 m, the giant car on pages 2-3 is 10 paces long. The ship on pages 18-19 is over 400 paces long (200 metres).

• Role play: ask the reader to imagine driving a giant machine, e.g. climbing up into cab of truck, sailing in a submarine or flying a jumbo jet.

© Aladdin Books Ltd 2008

Designed and produced by
Aladdin Books Ltd
PO Box 53987
London SW15 2SF

First published in 2008
by Franklin Watts
338 Euston Road
London NW1 3BH

Franklin Watts Australia
Level 17/207 Kent Street
Sydney, NSW 2000

All rights reserved
Printed in Malaysia

A catalogue record for this book is available from the British Library.

Dewey Classification: 621.8

ISBN 978 0 7496 8623 9

Franklin Watts is a division of Hachette Children's Books, an Hachette Livre UK company.
www.hachettelivre.co.uk

Series consultant
Zoe Stillwell is an experienced Early Years teacher currently teaching at Pewley Down Infant School, Guildford.

Photocredits:
l-left, r-right, b-bottom, t-top, c-centre, m-middle
All photos from istockphoto.com except: 2-3, 6-7, 10-11, 20br, 22br, 23bl & bmr — US Navy. 4-5, 23br – Vladimir Lukovic/Dreamstime.com. 8-9, 22tr, 23ml – US Army. 14, 23tr – NASA. 15 – Corbis. 18-19, 23tmr – courtesy Regent Seven Seas cruises.